Pine Lake

by David Sipes
illustrated by Ellie Cotton

Decodable 23

McGraw Hill Education

Bothell, WA • Chicago, IL • Columbus, OH • New York, NY

MHEonline.com

Send all inquiries to:
McGraw-Hill Education
8787 Orion Place
Columbus, OH 43240

ISBN: 978-0-02-143339-1
MHID: 0-02-143339-9

Printed in China

9 10 11 12 13 DSS 28 27 26 25 24

I am Kate.

I am on a little trip.

A Drive

Dad drives all of us.

Jim naps a little.

Mom said, "We can do lots at Pine Lake."

Hike and Bike

All of us hike.

We ride bikes to Pine Lake.